SECRETS OF THE SEASHORE

Carron Brown

Illustrated by Alyssa Nassner

A rock pool is bustling with life.

If you look closely between the rocks, beneath fronds of seaweed, and on the sandy bed, you will spot the animals living there.

Shine a torch behind the page, or hold it up to the light to reveal what is hidden in and around the rock pool. Discover a small world of great surprises.

A rock pool is a hollow
on the seashore.

Can you see what
happens when the tide
comes in?

Whoosh! The sea water flows in with the tide and fills the rock pool.

Creatures that live in sea water have waited for the rock pool to fill.

What's hiding in these shells?

Bubble...
Bubble...

Mussels keep their blue shells tightly
shut while the tide is out.

Now they open their shells and begin to feed.

Creatures cling to the rocks around the pool.

Who could live in shells like these?

Barnacles come to life
in the water. They reach out
their feathery legs to wave
tiny pieces of food
into their mouth.

Flutter flutter

Other creatures are waking up, too.

What are these jewel-like animals?

Stretch!

Two anemones are searching for food
with their long, wriggly tentacles.

They eat small fish and shrimp.

Dark nooks under rocks
make perfect hiding places.

Can you see who is resting here?

Clack!
Clack!

A crab holds its pincers up,
ready to grab a tidbit to eat.

The crab is on the move,
but there's another
hunter nearby.

Hold tight!

A starfish uses tube-like suckers on its underside to hold on to the rock.

Another animal with suckers
is resting in the rock pool.

Can you count its eight arms?

An octopus has eight long arms
with suckers on the underside.

It crawls slowly over the rocks.

There is an animal hiding in the sand.
Only its eyes can be seen.

What do you think it is?

Splish
Splash

A small fish lives in the rock pool.

It hides under rocks,
in seaweed and in the sand.

Another rock pool creature
lives in this large shell.

What do you think it could be?

Surprise!

A hermit crab has made his home
in the empty shell.

This whelk is
sharing its part of the
rock pool with small
swimming creatures.

Can you see them?

Skoosh!

Shrimp move backwards
with a quick flick of
their tail.

Their see-through bodies are much
easier to spot when they move.

Something is
waving in the water.

Which plants live
in the sea?

Slick and slimy seaweed
anchors itself to rocks
and grows in the sun.

What is slithering along
in the seaweed?

A whelk is looking for other shellfish.

It can drill a hole through a shell to eat the creature inside.

A sleek sea otter has spotted something.

Can you see what she wants for dinner?

Ouch!

Most animals stay away
from those nasty spikes,
but a sea urchin is a tasty
meal for the sea otter.

Which orange-beaked bird
lives on the seashore?

An oystercatcher is
calling out to other birds.

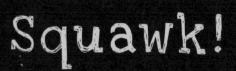

Squawk!

Can you see what the oystercatcher has found in the sand?

It's a clam!

The oystercatcher's long beak is perfect for finding buried food.

Slowly, the tide retreats,
and with it much of the
water in the rock pool.

Its animals and plants
are resting again, waiting
for the next tide to come in.

There's more...

When you find a rock pool, look all around it and see what you can spot. Remember to look under the seaweed and in dark places.

In the sand Clams have a soft body inside two joined shells. They burrow under the sand and push a feeding tube into the water. Clams pull in the tubes and snap their shells shut when they are in danger.

Stuck fast Whelks are sea snails that feed under water. When the tide goes out, they pull their body into their shell. They seal themselves in with a sticky substance that also sticks them to the rock.

In the cracks Crabs visit rock pools to feed on the animals there. They catch them with their large pincers. Walking under seaweed and resting in cracks keeps crabs hidden from hungry birds.

From the air Gulls fly down to rock pools and catch shelled creatures in their beaks. They fly up high then suddenly drop the shell on to rocks. This cracks the shell so that the birds can eat the soft meat inside.

Breaking in Sea otters grab sea urchins and shelled creatures from rock pools. To get at the meat inside, they float on their backs with the caught animal on their tummy and use a stone to crack open the shell.

Trapped The fish in rock pools are often the young of larger fish that live in shallow sea water. They are trapped in the pools when the tide goes out. They hide in the sand, and under seaweed and rocks.

Holding on Seaweed anchors itself to rocks with a root-like holdfast. Its fronds float towards the surface of the rock pool, and make food from sunlight. Many rock pool animals feed on seaweed.

Changing colour Octopuses can be hard to see because they can change colour to match their surroundings. They can also position their bodies so that they look like rocks or the rock pool floor.

Filtering Lots of rock pool creatures get their food by filtering it from the sea water. Each time the rising tide refills the rock pool, it brings with it fresh nutrients and food for the creatures that live there.

First published in the UK in 2014.
This edition published in 2015 by

Ivy Kids

An imprint of The Quarto Group
The Old Brewery
6 Blundell Street
London N7 9BH
United Kingdom
www.QuartoKnows.com

British Library Cataloguing-in-Publication Data
A catalogue record for this book is available from the British Library.

ISBN: 978-1-78240-236-7

This book was conceived, designed & produced by

Ivy Kids

58 West Street, Brighton BN1 2RA, United Kingdom

CREATIVE DIRECTOR Peter Bridgewater
MANAGING EDITOR Hazel Songhurst
COMMISSIONING EDITOR Georgia Amson-Bradshaw
ART DIRECTOR Kim Hankinson
DESIGNER Glyn Bridgewater
& Kim Hankinson

Printed in China

7 9 10 8 6

FSC
www.fsc.org
MIX
Paper from
responsible sources
FSC® C001701